I0463751

Murder

(including *actus reus* and *mens rea*)

Part of *The Law Explained* series

Sally Russell LLB (Hons), PGCE

My main objective has been to combine legal accuracy with a style that is accessible to all students, so I hope you will find this book both stimulating and helpful. Fully updated with recent cases and laws it is written in a lively, clear and accessible way and is designed to help students of all learning styles to understand the subject.

Although aimed at A-Level the books provide a good base for 1st Year LLB, ILEX and other courses, and can be used as self-study guides.

Each Chapter contains **examples** to help you see how the law relates to real life situations; **tasks** and **self-test questions**, to help you check your understanding, as well as **examination tips** and **application practice** to help you prepare for problem questions. Where applicable the books also contain **tips and guidance on evaluating** the law to help with essay questions. **Summaries** and **diagrams** help to make the law clear and the **'must-know' cases are highlighted**. Answers are given for the tasks and self-test questions either in the book or on my website at www.drsr.org

The *'the law explained'* series offers a more in-depth coverage of individual areas with additional tasks, examples and examination practice. This means you can pick those topics for which you need more guidance (all the answers are included in the book).

For a range of free interactive exercises please go to www.drsr.org and click on 'Free Exercises' to see what's available.

Other books by Sally Russell

As new books may be available by the time you read this I have not listed my other books by title. They currently include crime and tort at AS level, crime, tort and concepts of law for both the AQA and OCR examination board at A2 level and various books in *'the law explained'* series. For the most up to date list of what is available please check my author's page on Amazon or visit my website at www.drsr.org. All my books are available in both Kindle and paperback format.

About the author

Sally Russell was formerly head of law at a sixth-form college, a senior examiner for AQA and tort advisor for the Institute of Legal Executive Tutorial College. She has written various materials for both teachers and students, for Pearson Education, Hodder education and the National Extension College. She is also a regular contributor to the A-Level Law Review. For more information visit www.drsr.org

Contents

Introduction to Murder

Most offences require *actus reus* and *mens rea*. *Actus reus* is significant in murder cases because it is a result crime, so causation is important. *Mens rea* is what makes killing murder rather than manslaughter. I have therefore also covered these issues as far as they relate to murder. Don't be tempted to skip these if you did them for AS. You will have a good base to build on, but you need more depth to your knowledge at this level so concentrate on developing and evaluating what you know.

Examples

In **White**, D put cyanide in his mother's drink intending to kill her, but she died of a heart attack unconnected with the poison. He was not guilty of murder because although he intended to kill her, so had *mens rea*, the *actus reus* was not complete because his act didn't cause her death.

In **Hancock & Shankland,** the Ds threw a boulder at a taxi but as they did not intend either death or serious injury, the *mens rea* for murder was not present. They were guilty of manslaughter but not murder.

The tasks are intended to reinforce your learning so do these as you go along. The answers are at the end of the book. Some tasks will just ask you to jot down a few thoughts for use in an essay question, so there are no answers to these, but keep your notes for revision and exam practice. I have included occasional quotes so use these too; they show that you know what judges have to say about the law.

There are also some free interactive exercises at www.drsr.org

Criminal cases are usually in the form *R v the defendant*. It is acceptable to use just the name so if the case is **R v Miller** I have called it **Miller**. If another form is used, e.g., **DPP v Miller** I have used the full title, as you may want to look up the case for further information.

Civil cases are between the *claimant* and the *defendant*, although you will see the word *'plaintiff'* in cases before 1999.

There is a list of some common abbreviations in the appendix at the end of the booklet.

"... there was gross and criminal negligence, as the man was paid to keep the gate shut and protect the public ... a man might incur criminal liability from a duty arising out of a contract".

Wright J

The two elements which need to be proved for most offences are known by the Latin terms *actus reus* and *mens rea*. *Mens rea* involves the state of mind of D **at the time of the offence** so must coincide with the *actus reus*.

Coincidence of actus reus and mens rea

Although *actus reus* and *mens rea* must coincide, the court may view the *actus reus* as continuing. In **Fagan v Metropolitan Police Commissioner 1969**, D accidentally drove onto a police officer's foot whilst parking. He didn't move his car when asked to, and was convicted of assaulting a police officer in the execution of his duty. He argued that there was no *mens rea* at the time of the act (driving onto his foot). The court held that there was a continuing act. This started with driving onto the police officer's foot and continued up to the refusal to move. Thus, not moving when asked to was part of the original act and at this time, he did have *mens rea*. The courts have applied a similar rule to murder cases.

In **Thabo Meli 1954**, the Ds attacked a man planning to kill him. They then rolled what they thought was his dead body over a cliff, to make it look like an accident. He was only unconscious at this point, and the actual cause of death was exposure. The Ds were convicted of murder and argued that there were two separate acts. The first act (the attack) was accompanied by *mens rea* but was not the cause of death (so no *actus reus*). The second act (pushing him over the cliff) was the cause of death, but was not accompanied by *mens rea*. The *mens rea* of murder is intention to kill or seriously injure. They said there could be no such intention if they thought that the man was already dead. The court said that it was *"impossible to divide up what was really one series of acts in this way"*, and refused their appeal.

Actus reus involves everything else (other than the mental element) which makes up the crime, so we will look at this first.

Actus reus may include:

conduct (which is voluntary)

circumstances

a consequence (which is caused by D's conduct)

It is very important to identify each element of the *actus reus* of a crime because there can be no crime unless the *actus reus* is complete. This does not necessarily mean D will be acquitted. If part of the *actus reus* of an offence is not proved then *that* offence is not committed, but there may well be a connected offence or an attempt.

Example

In **White 1910**, D put cyanide in a drink intending to kill his mother. She died of a heart attack unconnected with the poison. The *actus reus* was not complete because his act didn't cause her death (more on this case below with causation). He was not guilty of murder, but was guilty of attempted murder.

Conduct

As a rule, the conduct must be voluntary. This is seen in **Leicester V Pearson 1952**, where a car driver was prosecuted for failing to give precedence to a pedestrian on a zebra crossing. It was shown that his car had been pushed onto the crossing by another car hitting him from behind. He was acquitted because he had not acted voluntarily.

Conduct can consist of an act, an omission, or a state of affairs. An **act** is usually straightforward, e.g., hitting someone. An **omission** is a failure to act. In criminal law, this will not usually make you guilty unless you have a duty to act in the first place. An example is failing to look after your child. A **state of affairs** is where you can commit an offence just by being in a certain state, e.g., 'being *drunk* in charge of a motor vehicle'.

A case illustrating the distinction between an act and an omission is **Airedale NHS Trust v Bland 1993**. Tony Bland, who was 17, had been badly injured in the Hillsborough football stadium disaster. He was in what is called a persistent vegetative state and had no hope of recovery. The family and doctors wanted to stop treatment, including artificial feeding. The HL confirmed a court order allowing this. They drew a distinction between a positive act that killed (such as administering a lethal injection) which could never be lawful, and an omission to act which allowed someone to die (e.g., not providing life-saving treatment).

The cases of **Diane Pretty** and **Ms B** in **2002** also illustrate this distinction. In the first, Mrs Pretty wanted her husband to help her commit suicide and took her case to the HL and then the European Court of Human Rights. She wanted a court order that he would not be prosecuted for assisting her suicide. She failed, as this would be a positive act. In the latter case, Ms B wanted treatment discontinued and succeeded in obtaining a court order to allow this, even though it meant she would die.

So, there is generally no criminal liability for *not* doing something. However, exceptions occur when there is a duty to act. A duty can occur when:

Parliament has expressly provided for it by statute

there is a contractual duty

a relationship of responsibility gives rise to a common law duty

D has created a dangerous situation

In these cases, an omission to act is enough.

Example

You see someone drowning and you are a good swimmer, but leave them to die. You are not guilty of any crime. However, as I said above there are exceptions. I will come back to this example as we look at the exceptions.

Statutory duty to act

An example is the **Road Traffic Act 1988**, which makes it an offence for a driver involved in a road accident to fail to stop and give a name and address when asked, or to fail to report the accident to the police. There is a duty to stop, and to report the accident, so failing to do so (an omission) is part of the *actus reus* of each of these offences.

Contractual duty to act

In **Pittwood 1902**, D was employed as a gatekeeper by a railway company. His job was to keep the gate at the crossing shut whenever a train passed. One day he forgot to close the gate. A hay cart crossed the track and was hit by an oncoming train. One person was killed and another seriously injured. D was under a contractual duty of employment to keep the gates to the crossing shut and to safeguard people using the crossing. His failure to act was in breach of his contractual duty and so he was guilty of manslaughter. If he had left the gate open knowing someone was about to cross he could have been guilty of murder as there would be intent to kill. The quote at the beginning came from this case.

In my example, if you were a lifeguard you would have a contractual duty to act so could be liable.

Relationship of responsibility

In **Stone and Dobinson 1977**, a couple had a relative (Fanny) come and live with them. She was anorexic, and often took to her bed for days at a time, refusing food and any other form of assistance. Her condition seriously deteriorated and after inadequate efforts to obtain medical assistance, she was found dead in her bed. The court held that Stone and Dobinson had undertaken the duty of caring for her and they had been grossly negligent in their failure to fulfil their duty. This failure had caused Fanny's death and so they were guilty of manslaughter. The same applies to murder. In **Gibbins and Proctor 1918**, a similar case resulted in a conviction for murder. Here the D's lived together with the man's daughter. They failed to give her food and she died. The court held that where food was withheld with intent to cause grievous bodily harm then it would be murder if this caused death. The CA upheld their murder convictions.

In my example, if you were the parent of the swimmer or if you had taken on responsibility for them, you would have a duty to act so could be liable.

Creating a dangerous situation

In **Miller 1983**, D was squatting in an unoccupied house. One night he fell asleep whilst smoking. When he awoke he realised he'd set fire to the mattress but did nothing to extinguish it, he merely moved to another room. The house caught fire and damage was caused. He was convicted of arson under **s 1 Criminal Damage Act 1971**. The HL upheld his conviction on the basis that if someone has unintentionally caused an event, and then realises what has happened, there is a duty to take appropriate action. This could also apply to murder if it was done with intent and someone died.

In my example, if you pushed them in, you created the dangerous situation so have a duty to take appropriate action. Again, you could be liable.

Task 1

Compare **Fagan** and **Miller**. Could Miller have been found guilty on the 'continuing act' theory?

Essay pointer

Think about whether there should be liability for omissions. Use the above cases to support your arguments. There is no 'right' answer. It can be argued that there is a moral duty to act if it will save a life. Consider whether there should also be a legal duty. Do you think the court made the right decision in the Tony Bland case? It can be said that turning off the machine was an act, but the court viewed it as an omission. On the other hand, in **Fagan,** it could be said there was only an omission but the court found a 'continuing act'. Do you think judges have too much discretion, e.g., to distinguish precedents? Is it better to have certainty in the law or to ensure justice is done in a particular case?

Circumstances

Many crimes are committed only if the conduct is carried out in particular circumstances. For murder, there must be an 'unlawful' killing. If, for example, D acted in self-defence then in these circumstances the act is not unlawful. The *actus reus* is not satisfied.

Task 2

Make a separate folder for the more detailed material you need for essays. As you read cases start to question what is satisfactory – or not – about the law and add your thoughts to the folder. Look out for articles from newspapers or law journals on any of the issues you are discussing. Cut them out and put them in the folder, adding a few of your own comments.

Consequences and causation

Crimes where a particular consequence is part of the *actus reus* are called **result crimes**. Murder is an example. For a murder conviction, death must result from D's act. Homicide is the unlawful killing of a human being. The *actus reus* involves not just killing (conduct) but also that it is unlawful and of a human being (circumstances) and that death occurs (the consequence).

As well as the consequence itself, it must be proved that D's act *caused* this consequence. Many of the cases on causation involve a homicide because homicide is a result crime. The prosecution must prove causation both **factually** and **legally**.

Factual causation

Factual causation is traditionally referred to as the *'sine qua non'* rule. This phrase is defined in Chambers as 'an indispensable condition'. It means D's action must be a *'sine qua non'* or an 'indispensable condition' of the result. More simply put, the result would not have occurred without D's action. It is more commonly called the 'but for' test. For murder the prosecution must show that 'but for' D's conduct, the victim would not have died.

Key case

In **White 1910**, D put cyanide in a drink intending to kill his mother, who was found dead shortly afterwards with the drink 3 parts full. In fact, the mother had died of a heart attack unconnected with the poison. The son was found not guilty of murder. He had the *mens rea* (he intended to kill her) but not the *actus reus* (his act didn't cause her death). He was guilty of attempted murder, however.

White illustrates the situation where D's act has *not* factually caused death. Any of the following cases on legal causation could also be used to illustrate causation in fact. As you read them, ask the question: 'but for D's act would the victim have died / been injured?' If the answer is 'no' then causation in fact is shown. Causation in fact can be very wide.

Example

I ask a college student to stay on for half an hour to finish a project. She therefore misses her bus and walks home. On the way, she is attacked and injured. It can be argued that 'but for' my asking her to stay late she would not have been attacked and so I am liable for her injury. To avoid such a wide liability the courts have built up some rules on how far someone should be liable for the consequences of their actions. This is causation in law.

Legal causation

This is based on what is called the 'chain of causation'. It means proving an unbroken link, or chain, between D's action and the result, for example, death in homicide cases. When something has occurred after D's original act, then it may be argued that the chain of causation is broken. We will look at some cases to explain how this works, but in summary; the chain of causation will not be broken if:

> *D's action makes a 'significant' contribution to the result (Smith/Cheshire)*
>
> *any intervening act was foreseeable (Roberts)*

the victim has a particular weakness and the result would not have occurred in a normal person (known as the 'thin skull' rule (Blaue))

In my example, I will argue that the chain has been broken by the attacker. I did not make a significant contribution to the harm, and the attack was not foreseeable. I have not legally caused the injuries.

Task 3

Use my example above, but this time apply it to the attacker. Decide whether the attacker legally caused death in the following situations:

1. The attacker left her badly injured and lying in the road. She is run over by a car and killed.

2. The attacker left her badly injured, but a passer-by sees her and calls an ambulance. In hospital, she starts to recover but the doctors give her the wrong drugs and she dies.

3. She was only slightly injured but (not a good day!) she is struck by lightning as she recovers from the attack.

We will come back to this, but first we'll look at some cases.

In **Smith 1959**, a soldier stabbed in a fight was dropped twice on the way to the treatment centre and then left untreated for some time. Although the court recognised that this contributed to the death, they found Smith, who had stabbed him, guilty of murder. As Lord Parker LCJ put it, his act was *"still an operating cause and a substantial cause"* of the death. A case where D's act was *not* found to have caused the death in similar circumstances is **Jordan 1956**. Here the stab wounds were healing well, but the doctor gave the victim treatment which caused an allergic reaction from which he died. The doctor's act was found to have broken the chain of causation. It is more likely that **Smith** will be followed nowadays, as in the next case.

Key case

In **Cheshire 1991**, due to negligent treatment by the hospital, complications arose after an operation on the victim of a shooting. The victim subsequently died. The person accused of the murder argued that his act had not caused the death of the victim; the hospital had done so. The court rejected the argument, following **Smith**. They said that as long as D's action was a 'significant and operative' cause of the death it need not be the sole cause. The jury should not regard hospital treatment as excluding D's responsibility unless it *"was so **independent of his acts**, and in itself so **potent in causing death**, that they regard the contribution made by his acts as insignificant."*

This principle was followed by the CA in **Mellor 1996**. An elderly man was taken to hospital following an attack in which he suffered broken ribs and other injuries. He died from bronchial-pneumonia brought on by his injuries. The hospital had failed to give him oxygen which may have saved him, but D was found guilty of murder. These cases show that the courts are reluctant to allow medical treatment to break the chain of causation and thus prevent D being found guilty

In **Pagett 1983**, D armed himself with a shotgun and took a pregnant girl hostage in a flat. Armed police called on him to come out. He eventually did so, holding the girl in front of him as a human shield. He then fired the shotgun at the police officers who returned fire, killing the girl hostage. The actions of the police did not break the chain because shooting back at D was held to be a 'natural consequence' of his having shot first. D was convicted of manslaughter, but if he had had the *mens rea* of intent, he would have been guilty of murder.

See also **Gnango 2011,** discussed below with murder where the chain of causation was broken in similar circumstances.

Key Case

In **Roberts 1971**, D – in a moving car – committed an assault on the victim by trying to take off her coat. She jumped out and was injured. He was charged with actual bodily harm. The court had to decide whether the assault caused the injury, or whether her actions broke the chain of causation. It was held that only if it was something that no reasonable person could foresee would the chain of causation be broken by the victim's actions. Here this was not the case so he was liable for her injuries. This means a magistrate or jury may take into account that the victim may do the wrong thing on the spur of the moment.

The same rule applies to homicide. In **Corbett 1996**, the victim was trying to escape an attack by D, when he fell and was hit by a car and died. His action came within a foreseeable range of consequences so did not break the chain.

A final point: it was recognised in **Roberts** that V might do the wrong thing in the agony of the moment. In **Williams & Davis 1992**, the CA said that only if V does something "*so daft or unexpected*" that no reasonable person could be expected to foresee it, would the chain of causation be broken.

Before looking at the final rule on causation, what did you decide in the task? Remember legal causation turns on how significant a contribution the attack made and whether the 'intervening act' (the car, the hospital treatment or the lightning) was foreseeable. You can therefore ask:

> *Whether it is foreseeable that a car will come along and hit her – yes, she is lying in the road. The chain is not broken by the car.*

> *Whether it is foreseeable that hospital treatment may be inappropriate – yes, it happens enough for it to be foreseeable. The chain is not broken by the hospital treatment.*

> *Whether it is foreseeable that she is struck by lightning – not likely, it is very rare. In addition, as she was only slightly injured, the attack did not make a significant contribution. The chain is broken by the lightning.*

Note that in the last one this does not mean the attacker gets off. He will still be liable for the attack, but not the death.

Summary

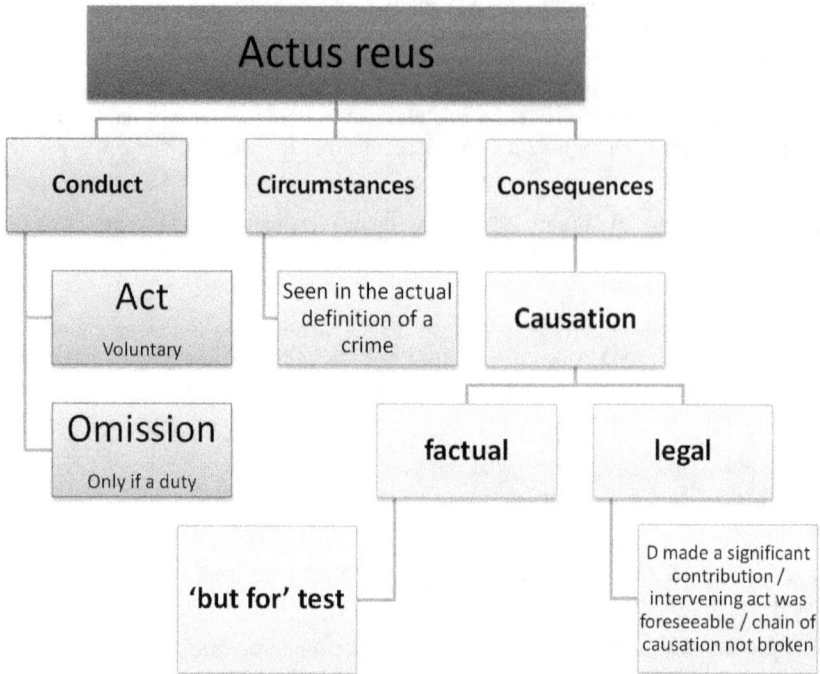

Essay pointer

If you were on the jury, would you know what acts should be considered 'independent' or 'potent' enough to break the causation chain? How significant is significant? What amounts to a 'daft' act by the victim? There may be a thin line between doing 'something wrong in the agony of the moment' and doing something 'daft'.

The 'thin skull' rule

A final issue on causation is that the chain is not broken by a particular vulnerability in the victim. Lawton LJ said in **Blaue 1975**, "*those who use violence on other people must take their victims as they find them*". Also known as the 'thin-skull rule', this appears to conflict with the 'foreseeability' rule. If a particular disability in the victim means that they are more likely to be harmed, or die, D is still liable even though V's act was not foreseeable.

Key case

In **Blaue 1975**, Lawton LJ went on to say, "*This in our judgement means the whole man, not just the physical man*". The victim was stabbed repeatedly and rushed to hospital where doctors said she needed a blood transfusion to save her life. She was a Jehovah's Witness and so refused to have one. She consequently died. D was convicted of manslaughter, though he stabbed her several times so it could easily have been murder. The 'disability' is more often physical (like a pre-existing medical condition such as a 'thin skull') but here it was the fact that she was a Jehovah's Witness.

Examination tip: problem questions

In a problem question, look out for anything that D can argue broke the chain. For example, D attacks someone and, as they are running away, they are hit by a car or bus. **Roberts** can be used to say that this is unlikely to break the chain. Look out for words like 'near the road' or 'in the bus station'. These suggest it is foreseeable. If V refuses treatment, you may need the 'thin-skull' rule.

Here look out for the reason. If it is a completely idiotic decision, then **Blaue** may be distinguished. If it is due to religious beliefs, it will be followed.

Examination tip: evaluation questions

All the matters in the essay pointers are ones which can be discussed in an evaluation essay, using the cases to illustrate what you say. There are usually valid arguments on both sides so don't strive to write what you think examiners want to see; they will be much more impressed with a balanced argument. Have an opinion, but look at the issue from the other point of view too. This shows you have considered the arguments before reaching your own opinion.

Task 4

Draw a diagram for *actus reus* like the one above for your files. Add a case to each of the principles and keep it as a revision guide.

Mens rea

The term *mens rea* refers to the state of mind of the accused at the time the *actus reus* is committed. As we saw, *mens rea* and *actus reus* must exist at the same time.

The two main types of *mens rea* are intention and recklessness. Only the first applies to murder.

It is important to be able to identify both the *actus reus* and the *mens rea* of the offence when answering a problem question. Each and every part of a crime has to be proved beyond reasonable doubt (as we saw in **White**, if all the elements are not proved D is not guilty of the offence).

Many cases dealing with intention are homicide cases because intention differentiates murder from manslaughter. The *mens rea* for murder is an intention to kill or seriously injure someone (**DPP v Smith 1960**). Intention can be direct or oblique (indirect).

Direct Intent

Direct intent means the result is D's aim or purpose. This is what most of us would understand by intention. If you pick up a loaded gun and fire it at someone with the aim of killing them, it can be said without any difficulty that you intended to do so. Intention was defined in **Mohan 1975** as 'the decision to bring about' the result, or prohibited consequence, whether that result was desired or not. The courts have given the concept of intention a wider meaning, however. This is referred to as oblique, or indirect, intent.

Oblique intent

The consequence isn't your aim but is 'virtually certain' to occur as a result of your actions.

Example

One night, two animal rights activists set fire to a shop which sells fur coats. The shop is closed but a security guard dies in the fire. Are they guilty of murder? They do not have the *mens rea* of *direct* intent, as their purpose is to make a political point, not to kill. They may have *oblique* intent. This will depend on the evidence. We will come back to this. For now, just make a note of what you think.

The issue of intent has been problematic (so a good source of material for evaluation of the law). **S 8 Criminal Justice Act 1967** provides that the jury *"shall not be bound in law to infer that D intended or foresaw a result of his actions by reason only of its being a natural and probable consequence of those actions"*. It also requires the jury to refer to *"all the evidence, drawing such inferences from the evidence as appear proper in the circumstances"*.

Example

11

Don fires a gun. The bullet kills someone. So, according to **s 8** what do the jury have to do?

The first bit means that just because it's likely to happen, it does not mean that the jury should infer that D intended it to happen. If Don fired into a crowded room, the jury may think death is a likely result, but this is *not enough by itself* to *prove* that Don intended it.

The second bit means that the jury must look at everything else. Where did it happen? What time of day was it? Did Don know there were people about? This will help them to decide what Don 'intended'. There is a difference between firing a gun into the air in the middle of an empty field and doing the same thing in a schoolroom. Even in the latter case, it may be that the school is closed and Don is the caretaker shooting at a rat not realising anyone is about. There is no answer which will always be right. That's what juries are for.

There has been a long line of cases on intent. Words like 'foreseeable', 'probable', 'likely' and 'natural' have all been used along the way. In **Smith 1960**, the HL had said that whether a result was probable was an objective test (what the reasonable person would "*contemplate as the natural and probable result*"). **S 8** makes the test subjective, whether the *defendant* saw it as probable. In **Hyam v DPP 1975**, a woman poured petrol through the letterbox of a rival and set fire to it. Two children died. She argued that she had only intended to frighten the other woman. The HL rejected her appeal but made clear the test was subjective. It was whether *she* saw the result as 'highly probable'. However, they also suggested that this was proof of intent, not just evidence of it. This point was rejected in **Moloney 1985**. It is now only a matter of evidence, not proof in itself.

In **Moloney**, D and his stepfather were having a drunken competition to see who could load and draw a shotgun the quickest. D won, and his stepfather said 'I didn't think you've got the guts, but if you have, pull the trigger.' D said he didn't aim the gun but just pulled the trigger. His murder conviction was quashed. The judge had directed the jury that they could find intent if D foresaw the result as 'probable' and the HL said that this was not enough; it needed to be a certainty. Lord Bridge explained intent in terms of 'moral certainty'. However, in his later summing up he said that a consequence was 'virtually certain' if it was a 'natural consequence'. This is not the same thing at all. Many 'natural' consequences are far from certain. Death from a lightning strike is a natural consequence of a storm, but not very likely – let alone certain!

In **Hancock and Shankland 1986**, two striking miners had pushed concrete blocks off a bridge to prevent a miner going to work. They said they only intended to scare him, but the driver of the taxi in which he was travelling was killed. Their conviction for murder was quashed. Both the CA and HL held that 'natural consequence' was misleading and that even awareness of the consequence as 'virtually certain' was only evidence and not proof of intent.

The law on oblique intent was clarified somewhat by the HL in **Woollin 1998**, which confirmed the direction given by the CA in **Nedrick 1986**.

The two key cases: Nedrick 1986 and Woollin 1998

In **Nedrick**, D poured paraffin through V's letterbox, circumstances not unlike those in **Hyam**, and set it alight. He said he only intended to scare her, but her child died in the resulting fire. He was convicted of murder and appealed based on lack of *mens rea*. The CA quashed his conviction because the jury had not been properly directed on intent. A conviction for manslaughter was substituted. In relation to oblique intent in a murder trial, the CA provided the following standard direction for the jury. Lord Lane said,

> "The jury should be directed that they are not entitled to infer the necessary intention unless they feel sure that death or serious bodily harm was a **virtual certainty** (barring some unforeseen intervention) as a result of the defendant's actions and that **the**

defendant appreciated that such was the case ... The decision is one for the jury to be reached on a consideration of all the evidence."

In **Woollin**, a father was convicted of murder after throwing his baby son across the room in a fit of temper. He argued that he had thrown the baby towards his pram but had not intended to kill him. His conviction was again substituted for one of manslaughter, this time by the HL. They confirmed the **Nedrick** direction and Lord Hope said. *"I attach great importance to the search for a direction which is both clear and simple ... I think that the **Nedrick** direction fulfils this requirement admirably"*

Thus, for murder, the two questions the jury must consider are:

+ **was death or serious bodily harm a virtual certainty?**

+ **did the defendant appreciate that such was the case?**

If the answer to both these questions is 'yes' then the jury may find intent. Although the HL used the word 'find' instead of 'infer', this seems of little import.

One other point. In some appeal cases, you may feel that the jury would have found intent. You could well be right. Many appeals are allowed because the jury was misdirected, not necessarily because intent could not be shown. The jury may have found sufficient evidence of intent, but were not directed correctly on the law.

Back to our example

If the defence can show that the two activists thought the shop was empty then the jury are unlikely to be convinced that they appreciated that anyone's death or serious injury was a virtual certainty. They could be convicted of manslaughter but not murder. If the prosecution can prove that they knew there was a guard on duty this will be evidence for the jury that they did appreciate that death or serious injury was a virtual certainty, so a conviction for murder is possible.

I have made both **Nedrick** and **Woollin** 'Key cases' because the law was *established* by the CA in **Nedrick**, but *confirmed* by the HL in **Woollin**, and a precedent carries greater weight once the HL has approved it. In addition, the **Nedrick** test has not been followed consistently. In **Walker and Hayles 1990**, although the CA held the test to be correct, they said that the use of the phrase 'a very high degree of probability' sufficed. More confusion! In **Woollin** itself, there was some confusion in the CA as to the application of the test (perhaps caused by the **Walker** decision). The Law Commission produced a report and **Draft Code** between the cases of **Nedrick** and **Woollin**, in which it gave a definition of intent. There was therefore some doubt as to whether, if a case reached the HL, the LC's definition would be preferred to the **Nedrick** one. Apparently not.

Essay pointer: Intention

The **Draft Code** definition is that D acts intentionally with respect to a result *"when he acts either in order to bring it about or being aware that it will occur in the ordinary course of events"*. In **Woollin**, Lord Steyn referred to the **Draft Code** but thought the **Nedrick** test was "very similar". It is arguable that the HL should have adopted the LC's definition if they thought it so similar. It seems quite clear and would become the law if the **Code** were ever adopted.

The test was followed again in **Matthews and Alleyne 2003**. The Ds had thrown V from a bridge into a river. He drowned. There was evidence that he had told them he couldn't swim. They appealed against their conviction for murder. The CA rejected their appeal but again said that foresight of death as a virtual certainty does not automatically prove intent, it is merely evidence (often very strong evidence) for the jury.

In **Stringer 2008**, D appealed against his convictions for both murder and arson with intent to endanger life. A fire had been started at the bottom of the stairs in his house, where several of his family were sleeping. His brother died. He had denied starting the fire. At the time he was 14 and had a low IQ. The CA accepted that when directing the jury on the question of intent based on **Woollin**, the judge did not make clear the distinction between the two parts of the test (the inevitability of death or injury, and D's appreciation of it). However, on the facts, there could be only one answer to the question whether it was a virtual certainty that somebody would suffer death or serious injury from a fire in these circumstances. As to the second part of the test, even taking account of his age and low IQ the judge said that,

> *"the inference that he must have appreciated it on that morning was also overwhelming. The jury's conclusion that [he] had the necessary intent was bound to follow"*

So firstly, death or serious injury was a virtual certainty, and secondly, he appreciated that this was the case. He therefore had indirect intent.

Examination tip

When applying the law you need only use **Nedrick** and **Woollin**, and only then in cases of oblique intent, not where it is direct intent. This was made clear in **Woollin**. D's knowledge will be an important factor. Look carefully at the facts for information such as 'they knew that ...' or 'unknown to them ...' These comments will help you to apply the test as in my example. The cases leading up to **Woollin** would be useful for an essay question on either *mens rea* or murder generally. A summary of these follows.

Summary of the development of the law on intent

Summary of the development of the law on intent

Case	Development	Probable, possible or certain?	Objective / subjective Proof or evidence
DPP v Smith 1960	HL held that the *mens rea* for murder is intention to kill or cause grievous bodily harm	Foresight of death or serious injury as a natural and probable result	Objective (what the 'reasonable man or woman' would contemplate)
Hyam 1974 (similar facts to Nedrick)	Changed to a subjective test by HL	Foresight of death or serious injury as highly probable	Noted that s8 had amended this to subjective It proved intent (this seems to contradict s8 which refers to evidence)
Moloney 1985	HL disapproved **Hyam** Foreseeing death as 'probable' was not proof of intent	Foresight of death or serious injury as a moral certainty or natural consequence	Foresight was *evidence* of intent rather than *proof* of intent
Hancock and Shankland 1986	**Moloney** guidelines were followed but HL held that 'natural consequence' was misleading	The greater the probability the more likely it was foreseen and thus intended	Evidence
Nedrick 1986	CA provided a new test	Death or serious injury was a virtual certainty and D appreciated this	Evidence from which the jury can 'infer' intent
Walker and Hayles 1990	CA followed **Nedrick** but added	very high degree of probability sufficed	Evidence from which the jury can 'infer' intent
Woollin 1998	HL confirmed **Nedrick** test	Death or serious injury was a virtual certainty and D appreciated this	Evidence from which jury can 'find' intent
Matthews and Alleyne 2003 / Stringer 2008	Applied **Nedrick** test	Death or serious injury was a virtual certainty and D appreciated this	Evidence of intent is not proof of intent

Task 5

Using the summary of the developments above, draw up a diagram and add a column to it. Use this column for a brief comment of your own, regarding either the principle or the facts. Keep the diagram as a guide for essays. It might look nice on the bedroom wall.

The other type of *mens rea* is recklessness. Subjective recklessness is used for most crimes as an alternative *mens rea* to intent. Objective recklessness was abolished by the HL in **Gemmell and Richards 2003**. For murder, however, recklessness is not enough, there must be intent to kill or seriously injure.

Transferred Malice

Mens rea can be transferred from the intended victim to the actual victim. This means that if you intend to hit Steve but miss and hit Joe you cannot say 'but I didn't intend to hit Joe so I had no *mens rea*'. In **Latimer 1886**, D aimed a blow at X with his belt but missed and seriously wounded V. He had the intent (*mens rea*) to hit X, and this intent was transferred to the wounding (*actus reus*) of V. Thus, he had both the *mens rea* and the *actus reus* of wounding. If V had died, the charge would have been murder; the same rule applies. However, the *actus reus* and *mens rea* must be for the *same* crime.

Example

I throw a brick at someone but it misses and breaks a window. I had *mens rea* for an assault and *actus reus* for criminal damage. This *mens rea* can't be transferred. I am not guilty of either crime. If I throw the brick at someone but it hits someone else then this *mens rea* can be transferred. I had *mens rea* and *actus reus* for the *same* offence.

Summary

Level of *mens rea*	Explanation	Cases	Example crimes
• Direct Intention	• D's aim or purpose, a decision to bring about the result	• Mohan 1975	• Murder, theft, grievous bodily harm and wounding with intent
• Indirect Intention	• Result is a virtual certainty and D appreciates this	• Nedrick 1986 CA • Woollin 1998 HL	• Murder, theft, grievous bodily harm and wounding with intent
• Subjective Recklessness	• D recognises a risk and goes on to take it	• Cunningham 1957	• All other assaults, criminal damage

Self-test questions

What '3 Cs' may be included in the actus reus of a crime?

*On what basis did the court find liability in **Fagan**?*

Give two examples of when an omission can result in criminal liability.

What is the thin skull rule?

From which case did the quote at the beginning of this Chapter come?

What are the two types of intent?

*What is the **Nedrick** test for oblique intent?*

*What is the principle in **Latimer**?*

For some free interactive exercises visit www.drsr.org and click on Free Exercises to see what's available

"... if at the time of death the original wound is still an operating cause and a substantial cause, then the death can properly be said to be the result of the wound, albeit that some other cause of death is also operating"

Lord Parker CJ

Can you remember in which case this statement was made? If not, look back at legal causation in Chapter 1.

There are definitions of murder going back to the 18th century and beyond. The most famous is that by Sir Edward Coke: 'the unlawful killing of a reasonable creature in being under the King's peace and with malice aforethought'. However, murder is a common law offence (not covered by an Act of Parliament), so the definition has changed through case law over time (for a start we now have a Queen not a King).

Actus reus

The *actus reus* is essentially the same for both murder and manslaughter. The modern definition of murder is the "**unlawful killing of a human being under the Queen's peace**".

Unlawful

Most killing will be unlawful. However, killing in self-defence may make the act lawful and so not murder.

Killing

People generally think of murder as involving an action (conduct) such as shooting or stabbing someone. However, murder can be committed by omission, as we saw in the case of **Gibbins and Proctor**.

The courts do draw a distinction between an act and an omission, however. In **Airedale NHS Trust v Bland 1993**, discontinuing medical treatment was treated as an omission rather than a positive action. This was a civil case so is not strictly binding on the criminal courts. It will be highly persuasive though. It can be compared to **Cox 1992**, where a doctor gave an injection to a patient begging for help to die. This is a positive act, and so amounts to murder. (On the facts, it was only attempted murder as the cause of death was not clear.) Intentionally accelerating death is still murder. Thus even if someone is about to die anyway you will be guilty of murder if you intentionally shorten their life. The only exception is what is known as the *de minimis* rule: if D's act is so small that it cannot be said to play a significant part in the death, there is no liability for murder.

Example

V is in severe pain from an incurable illness. The doctor gives her a huge overdose of painkillers in order to end her suffering. Before these take effect, V's husband gives her two more painkillers.

The doctor's act would be murder. The husband's act *could* be murder as it probably hastened the death, but the court might treat it as *'de minimis'*.

Essay pointer

Any intentional act which causes death will be murder. Thus 'mercy killing', or euthanasia, would be murder. You might argue that you were easing the suffering of someone incurably ill, but this argument will not succeed. Accelerating death is still murder. The motive for a crime is rarely relevant (it is as much theft to steal a loaf of bread for a starving child, as it is to steal a £5,000 music system). The motive could affect the sentence, but with murder, the judge has no choice in this.

This is why the **Bland** case went to the House of Lords. Without a court order, it could have been murder.

A related issue for an essay is the sentence for murder. One argument against a mandatory life sentence is that if the jury see the killing as morally justified they may be reluctant to find someone guilty of murder. They would know that it would mean a life sentence and that the judge would be unable to consider the circumstances. In 2005, the DPP, Ken Macdonald, recommended that a more flexible system should be introduced, similar to that in America, where there are different degrees of homicide. This change would mean that not all killings would be treated in exactly the same way, and could solve some of the difficulties for both judges and juries. The Law Commission has also recommended different levels of homicide but these suggestions have never been implemented.

Human being

This may seem obvious but questions arise about whether someone who is 'brain dead' or a foetus in the womb is a human being. In **AGs Reference (No 3 of 1994) 1997**, the HL held that a foetus was not a human being for the purpose of a murder conviction. However, if a foetus is injured, and dies from that injury after being born, that could amount to the murder of a 'human being'.

Under the Queen's peace

This part of the *actus reus* means that killing in war is not murder.

Causation

Murder is a result crime so it must be proved that death resulted from D's actions. If D caused death then the charge can be murder or manslaughter depending on the *mens rea*. If D did not cause death then it can only be one of the non-fatal offences or an attempt. We have seen that the prosecution must show **factual causation**: 'but for' the defendant's conduct the victim would not have died. Also **legal causation**: that D's act was a 'significant' cause of death and there was no intervening act.

Task 6

Before going any further, look up the following cases. Make a note of the facts.

White

Roberts

Smith

Cheshire

Pagett

Now make a note of the causation issue in each. Then read on to check these principles.

OK, let's briefly summarise the causation principles involved.

Factual causation

R v White 1910	'but for' his actions would she be alive? No, she would have died anyway so he did not cause that death.

Legal causation

R v Smith 1959	If D's act was an **operating and substantial** cause of death, there is no break in the chain of causation.
R v Cheshire 1991	Following **Smith**, if D has made a **significant contribution** to the death then hospital treatment will only break the chain of causation if it is **independent of the original act** and a potent cause in itself.
Roberts 1971 The prosecution relied on this case in **Corbett 1996**, to find that D caused the death of a victim who was hit and killed by a car when trying to escape from D's attack.	If the *victim's* act is **foreseeable**, it will not break the chain of causation, as long as it is not 'daft'.
R v Pagett 1983	If a *third party's* act is **foreseeable** it will not break the chain of causation and the police returning fire was a **natural consequence** of D's actions.

These cases could also be used to explain factual causation. In **Pagett** you would ask 'but for' his actions would she have died? No, so he factually caused death. (Note this test is sometimes reversed but the effect is the same: 'but for' his actions would she be alive? Yes, so he caused death.)

Essay pointer

If V is easily scared and therefore does something 'daft' this is arguably a vulnerability that is no different from having a thin skull or being a Jehovah's Witness, as in **Blaue**. **Blaue** itself is somewhat controversial. If the victim does not have a life-threatening injury but refuses treatment, should D be liable for the resulting death?

In **Gnango 2011**, two people had been involved in a shoot-out in a car park on a housing estate. The first man fired at D who shot back, the man then fired again and his bullet killed a woman nearby. The prosecution argued that in returning fire D had caused the other man to shoot again, so had also caused the woman's death. The SC held that, although it may have made it more likely that the man would shoot again, this was not enough. The voluntary act of the other man had broken any possible chain of causation between D's return of fire and the death. The other man alone had caused the death. This can be compared to **Pagett**, where it was found to be foreseeable that the police would return fire so the chain of causation was not broken. The main difference seems to be that in **Gnango** the victim was not being held by D as a hostage, but was merely walking nearby. Also, in **Pagett**, D shot first which was not the case in **Gnango**.

Mens rea

In Coke's 18th Century definition of murder, the unlawful killing must be done with '*malice aforethought*'. This expression is still used but has been interpreted as meaning with intention.

In **Vickers 1957**, the CA held that the *mens rea* for murder is satisfied by either an intention to kill, or an intention to cause grievous bodily harm. This was confirmed in **DPP v Smith 1960**, where the HL said that grievous bodily harm should be given its ordinary and natural meaning, that is to say, "*really serious bodily harm*". In **Saunders 1985**, it was said that the word 'really' did not add anything. Thus, the *mens rea* of murder is **intent to kill or seriously injure**. Intent can be direct or indirect as we saw in the last chapter.

Task 7

Look up the cases of **Nedrick** and **Woollin**. Make a note of the facts, and whether the murder charge succeeded, and why/why not.

Knowledge of the development of the law (set out in Chapter 1), is needed for a critique but, for a problem question, it is the current law that is important. We saw that this comes from the CA in **Nedrick 1986**. It was confirmed by the HL in **Woollin 1998** as being the correct direction for oblique intent. There is *evidence* of intent if:

death or serious bodily harm was a virtual certainty as a result of the defendant's actions

the defendant appreciated that such was the case

Key case

In **Woollin**, the jury had to consider whether D appreciated that it was a virtual certainty the baby would be killed or seriously injured by being thrown in the direction of the pram. The HL confirmed the point that this is only evidence of intention, not proof. The jury should be directed on the **Nedrick** test and told to take into account ALL the circumstances.

The test was followed again in **Matthews and Alleyne 2003**. The CA confirmed the test and also that foresight of death as a virtual certainty does not automatically *prove* intent; it is merely *evidence* (*"often very strong evidence"*) for the jury. The CA used the test again in **Stringer 2008** (see previous Chapter on *mens rea*). It would now appear to be the established test as **Nedrick** was over twenty years earlier.

Problems and reforms

In their 2006 report 'Murder, manslaughter and Infanticide' the Law Commission noted that

"The law governing homicide in England and Wales is a rickety structure set upon shaky foundations. Some of its rules have remained unaltered since the seventeenth century, even though it has long been acknowledged that they are in dire need of reform".

The LC recommended a three-tier structure for homicide, which would cover

1st-degree murder (killing with intent to kill or with intent to cause serious harm knowing the conduct carried a serious risk of death)

2nd-degree murder (killing with intent to cause serious harm or where there is a defence of provocation (now loss of control) or diminished responsibility as now for voluntary manslaughter) and

Manslaughter (killing without intent, as now for involuntary manslaughter but with mens rea *needed for some kind of harm)*

Only the first of these would have a mandatory life sentence. These recommendations have not been taken up.

Essay pointer

The *mens rea* of murder is intent to kill or seriously injure (**Smith 1960**). This means you can be guilty of murder even if you did not intend to kill. This point was confirmed in **Cunningham 1981** (not to be confused with the 1957 case of the same name on recklessness). The HL criticised the rule but has refused to overrule it in several cases, preferring to leave that to Parliament.

The Law Commission has also criticised the rule but no government has yet suggested amending the law. In **Attorney-General's Reference (No 3 of 1994) 1997**, the HL, although not overruling it, refused to apply it so as to find someone guilty of murder where there was only intent to cause serious injury, however this was a case of transferred malice so may be of limited application.

Murder is the most serious offence, so it is vital that the law is clear. Look at the development of intent in Chapter 1. Has it produced a clear meaning of intent? Pretend you are on a jury. Could you decide what degree of probability is virtually certain? The **Cunningham** test for recklessness is that D knowingly takes a foreseeable risk. The **Nedrick** test for intent is foresight of something as a virtual certainty. At what stage does a foreseeable risk become a certainty?

The above can be discussed in an essay question on *mens rea* or murder, or a more general one on homicide.

Intent and 'mercy killing'

In **Inglis 2010**, a mother was convicted of murder and sentenced to life imprisonment for killing her severely disabled son. There was clear intent to kill, so even though she acted in what she believed were her son's best interests the charge was murder. This can be compared with **Gilderdale** heard in the same week. Here a woman killed her daughter who had a chronic illness and who had tried to commit suicide herself on several occasions. She was cleared of attempted murder by a jury (attempted murder because it could not be shown if the drugs she gave caused the death or not). Again, she intended to kill her daughter so the charge had to be murder, but the jury were clearly sympathetic.

Essay pointer

These cases highlight the difficulties. Mrs Gilderdale was given a 12-month conditional discharge for aiding and abetting a suicide, whereas Mrs Inglis was given a life sentence for murder, even though there was little real difference in the facts and in both cases the mothers acted in what they believed was their child's best interests. The main difference seems to have been that in **Inglis** her son was too disabled to be able to communicate his own wishes, whereas in **Gilderdale** the daughter would probably have found a way to kill herself anyway. She had expressed a desire to end her life and this was taken into account by the jury, and by the judge when he said that the decision of the jury showed *"common sense, decency and humanity"*.

However, the huge contrast in sentencing in these cases shows the problem of having a mandatory life sentence where the judge has no discretion.

In their 2004 report 'Partial Defences to Murder' the Law Commission said

> *"the Government should undertake a public consultation on whether, and if so to what extent, the law should recognise either an offence of "mercy" killing or a partial defence of "mercy" killing".*

Making it a separate offence or a partial defence (as with diminished responsibility and loss of control) would allow for discretion in sentencing and perhaps make juries more willing to convict.

Summary of murder

| | • The unlawful killing of a human being |
| Actus reus | • Death is caused by D's act or omission both factually (**White**) and legally (**Cheshire/Roberts**) |

	• Direct intent - D's aim or purpose (**Mohan**)
	• Indirect intent - D saw the consequence as a virtual certainty (**Nedrick/Woollin**)
Mens rea	• to kill or seriously injure (**Vickers/Smith**)

Self-test questions

What is the actus reus *and* mens rea *of murder, and how have the courts interpreted the latter?*

What is a result crime and what is the significance in terms of actus reus?

Can you explain the law on causation using two murder cases?

In which CA case was the 'virtual certainty' test for mens rea *established, and which HL case confirmed this?*

For some free interactive exercises visit www.drsr.org and click on Free Exercises to see what's available

Key criticisms of *actus reus*, *mens rea* and murder

> *D is not usually liable for an omission but can be in certain circumstances, there is a degree of uncertainty in such cases e.g., Bland, Gibbins & Proctor.*

> *Sometimes questions arise about whether someone who is 'brain dead' or a foetus in the womb is a human being. In AGs Reference (No 3 of 1994) 1997, the HL held that a foetus was not a human being for the purpose of a murder conviction. However, if the foetus is injured, and dies from that injury after being born, that could amount to murder. Arguably, there should be greater clarity on this.*

> *The rules on what will break the chain of causation may be difficult for a jury to understand.*

> *The law on intent has developed but is arguably still unclear*

> *The mandatory life sentence for murder means the judge has no discretion and cannot take into account the very different circumstances between some killings, in euthanasia cases. A discretionary sentence could remove the need for the special defences (voluntary manslaughter) as the circumstances could be taken into account by the judge.*

> *Murder is a common law offence. Should there be a statutory definition? If so should it contain more than one degree of murder as in the USA (and as recommended by the Law Commission – see below)? This could again remove the need for the special defences.*

> *The mens rea for murder is intent to kill or seriously injure, for such a serious crime should it only be intent to kill?*

Reforms

In their 2006 report 'Murder, manslaughter and Infanticide' the Law Commission noted four particular problems with the law on homicide and said:

> *If excessive force is used in self-defence this should come within the partial defences (voluntary manslaughter)*

> *It is not right that duress cannot be a defence to murder in any circumstances*

> *The serious harm rule is wrong and there should be intent to kill, or at least intent to cause serious harm knowing there is a risk of death*

> *The two-category structure of murder or manslaughter is out-dated. The LC felt someone who killed, e.g., under provocation should still be called a murderer but should not have a life sentence. They recommended a three-tier structure for homicide, which would cover*

> 1st-degree murder

> 2nd-degree murder

> Manslaughter

Only the first of these would have a mandatory life sentence.

The LC also wanted a new **Homicide Act** not only to deal with the partial defences but also to clarify the law. They said that the new Act should provide clear and comprehensive definitions of the homicide offences and the partial defences.

These recommendations have not been taken up, although the self-defence issue is now covered by the 'fear of serious violence' trigger for loss of control in the **Coroners and Justice Act**.

Task 8

Using the essay pointers and key criticisms, write out a few paragraphs with your thoughts on the problems. Add a few cases in support and keep this for revision and examination practice.

A general guide to revision

The first and foremost rule for revision is to start early. Too many students leave it until the last minute and then get in a panic. If you take it gently and organise your time properly you will feel a lot more calm and confident when exam time comes. Make a plan of what you want to cover each day and try to stick to it. Don't forget to include some breaks in your schedule, if you are tired it will be harder to retain the material you have been revising.

Here are a few tips for revision techniques

> *Go through your notes and try to summarise them*
>
> *Learn the key cases, as these are essential to know*
>
> *Make sure you understand how the judge has applied the law to the facts so you can do the same in an examination scenario*
>
> *If the case is one you may also want to use in an essay, be sure you understand any problems it raises or solves and / or the concept of law that is involved*

Example

In **Brown**, the judges decided that consent was not a defence to serious harm, so this would apply to a scenario involving GBH.

It raises a problem in the law, because the reasoning was obscure. It was not sufficiently clear why the consent defence failed. It could be argued that the defence fails if harm was intended (this would apply to s 18 but not 20), or alternatively that the defence fails if harm was serious (this would apply to both s 18 and 20).

Another problem, and one which relates to the concept of law and morals, is that some of the judges seemed to rely on their own moral values when reaching their decision.

> *Go through the summaries of the topic, these provide a base of the essential points which may need to be addressed*
>
> *Go to the examination board's website for past exam papers, mark schemes and reports*
>
> *Practice answering questions then look at the examiners' mark schemes and reports to see if you were on the right track*

Revision of murder

Murder has the *actus reus* of an unlawful killing of a human being which causes death

Actus reus: conduct which is voluntary (killing), circumstances (unlawful and of a human being), consequence (D caused death)

The prosecution must prove causation both **factually** and **legally**.

Factually – the 'but for' test **White 1910**

Legally – D's action made a 'significant' contribution to the result (**Cheshire**) and any intervening act was foreseeable (**Roberts**)

The 'thin skull' rule – where V has a particular weakness D will be liable for the full consequences (**Blaue**)

Murder has the *mens rea* of intent to kill or seriously injure (**Smith**)

Intent can be:

Direct – where it is D's aim or purpose (**Mohan**) or

Indirect – where D appreciates death or serious injury as a virtual certainty (**Nedrick/Woollin**)

Example

Tom and Sam were involved in a shoot-out in a car park on a housing estate. Tom shot at Sam who fired back, Tom then fired again and his bullet killed a woman nearby. Who is liable for the death?

Both Tom and Sam had intent to seriously injure because even if not direct it is virtually certain that serious injury will result from a shoot-out and they would appreciate this (**Nedrick/Woollin**). They therefore had *mens rea*. Under the doctrine of transferred malice (**Latimer**) this *mens rea* can be transferred to the death of the woman. The woman died and the killing was unlawful so the remaining question regarding *actus reus* is one of causation. Tom's bullet hit the woman so he directly caused her death and it should not be hard to find him guilty of murder. The case of **Pagett** can be used to suggest that Sam could also be guilty if his firing back at Tom caused Tom to fire the final shot. This will apply only if Sam made a significant contribution to the death (**Cheshire**) and returning fire is seen as foreseeable. In **Pagett**, he held the girl in front of him so made a significant contribution to her death and it was foreseeable that the police might fire and the girl could get seriously hurt. Here Sam will probably not be guilty of murder because not only had he no connection to the woman, but also it was Tom who shot first (unlike in **Pagett**).

This example is based on the case of **Gnango 2011**. The prosecution had argued that in returning fire D had caused the other man to shoot again, so had also caused the woman's death. The SC held that, although it may have made it more likely that the man would shoot again, this was not enough. The voluntary act of the other man had broken any possible chain of causation between D's return of fire and the death. The other man alone had caused the death.

Examination tip

It is OK to say 'probably' in a conclusion. You can't be expected to play judge and jury. It is better than "D will be guilty (or not) of ..." – it is rarely that simple! Decide what seems most appropriate, and then use the law to prove it. You could conclude that D may be guilty of murder, but that as intent is hard to prove it may be manslaughter. Then you should go on to discuss involuntary manslaughter. However, read the question carefully. If you are *only* asked to discuss murder, don't go on to manslaughter.

Task 9

Briefly explain the following cases to show whether it was murder

> ***Gibbins and Proctor***
>
> ***Cheshire***
>
> ***Nedrick***
>
> ***White***

For some free interactive exercises visit www.drsr.org and click on Free Exercises to see what's available

Although different exam boards have different ways of styling their examination papers, there are always going to be common elements. You will need to be able to apply the law you have learnt to a particular scenario and you will need to be able to evaluate a given topic to provide a critique of the law, including reforms where appropriate.

A general guide to examination papers

Read **all** questions carefully before deciding which to answer

Look again at the ones you wish to answer to make sure you can do so, make brief notes - this can be a useful checklist later when you are tired and your memory begins to fail.

Structure your answer. Remember this is a test of law so you need to state the legal principles involved and apply them to the particular question. A solid start is worth a lot and gets the examiner on your side. A small plan is helpful.

It is necessary to do more than regurgitate your notes. You need to be selective as to what is relevant, and to choose appropriate cases and examples in support of what you say.

Never put in irrelevant material just because you know it - there is **never** a question asking you to 'write all you know about...'. The examiner wants to know that you understand the specific issues and can apply the appropriate law to the facts given.

Always support your answer with **relevant** cases. Don't worry too much about the facts, the principle forming the *ratio decidendi* is usually the important part e.g. in **Donoghue v Stevenson** that you owe a duty to others to take care is vital but you don't need to write a paragraph discussing snails and ginger beer.

Having said that, you want to show why you have chosen a particular case so will need to mention any facts that specifically relate to the scenario. If the scenario mentions someone being ill after consuming a chocolate bar with a dead mouse in it (yes, there has been a case!) then talking briefly about snails in ginger beer will be relevant. The main point here is that you need to be selective; this demonstrates a skill in itself and conserves precious time.

If you can't remember the name of a case that is relevant, don't leave it out but refer to it in a general way e.g. 'in one decided case....' or 'in a similar case....'

In problem questions, identify the various issues in the first paragraph and then set about dealing with them one by one, applying the relevant law and cases to each issue, **referring to the facts of the question as you do so**. This tells the examiner that you are answering the specific points raised. A short summing up is also a good idea e.g., "In conclusion it would appear that D may be liable for ... but it is possible that the defence of ... applies which will reduce/negate liability".

In essay questions, you will usually be asked to form an opinion or to weigh up arguments for and against a particular statement. Here a broader range of knowledge is needed showing arguments for, arguments against and an evaluation of these arguments. If reforms have been proposed or implemented, discuss these too. You should always round off your answer with a short concluding paragraph, preferably using some of the wording from the question to indicate to the examiner that you are addressing the specific issue raised.

Essays should have a logical structure. The beginning, should introduce the subject matter, the central part should explain/analyse/criticise it as appropriate, and the conclusion should bring the various strands of argument together with reference to the question set.

Try to consider alternative arguments. A well-rounded essay will bring in other views even if you disagree with them; you cannot shoot them down without setting them up first.

Essay writing is a skill in itself, so here is a brief guide on how to structure your essay.

Writing a discussion essay: staging the information logically

If you stage your essay as follows, it will make it easy to read, logically structured and easier to write. It may also mean you don't leave out important points. Here's how it works:

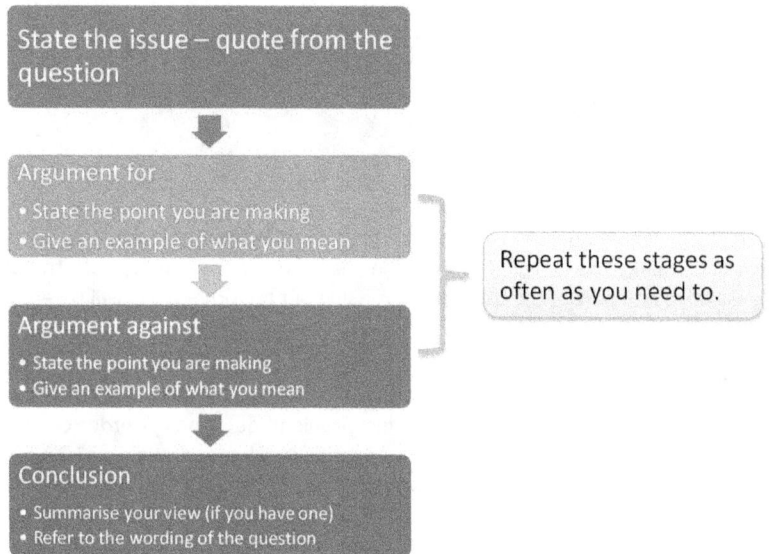

Writing each paragraph: making each one logical and easy to read (and write!)

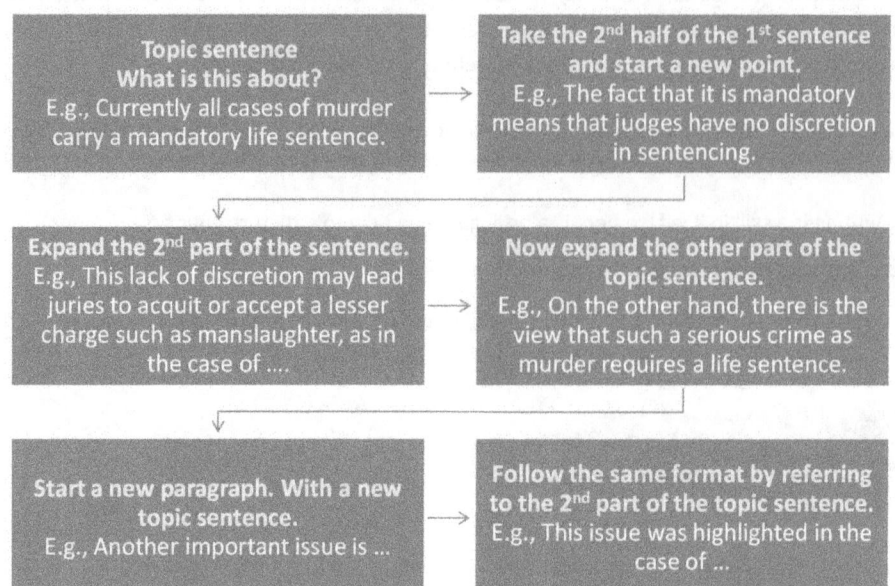

Finally, make sure you cover the whole question. For both problem and evaluation questions, there are only a certain number of marks available. The examiner has a mark scheme to work to, so however brilliant your answer to one part of the question is, missing out the other parts will severely reduce your total marks.

Problem scenarios (application)

The law on AR and MR prepares you for answering a murder 'problem' question. Murder can be committed by an omission (**Gibbins & Proctor**); it is a result crime so it must be proved that D's act caused death factually (**White**) and in law (**Cheshire/Roberts**). Murder requires the MR of intent (**Nedrick/Woollin**) to kill or seriously injure (**Smith**).

Application of the law requires you to be selective. The facts should point you to particular issues which need addressing and you must be prepared to pick out the relevant law and cases and to leave out anything irrelevant – for which you will gain no marks.

Examples

Gary fires a gun at Jon and kills him. Here there is an unlawful killing with intent at least to seriously injure Jon, so it is clearly murder. There are no issues regarding intent or causation so these can be dealt with very briefly. (In a case like this, where there is little to say about murder, the scenario will probably indicate evidence of diminished responsibility or loss of control so you would go on to discuss the special defences to murder, i.e., voluntary manslaughter).

Gary fires a gun at Jon and hits Annie instead, killing her. Here there is intent to kill and little problem with causation so these can be dealt with quickly. The issue is transferred malice (**Latimer**), so deal with this in more detail to explain the intent can be transferred from the intended victim (Jon) to the actual victim (Annie).

Gary fires a gun at Jon but misses. As Jon runs away he is hit by a car and killed. There is intent to kill so deal with this quickly and move on to the issue of causation. Use **Roberts** to suggest that running away from the attack is a foreseeable and reasonable action, so will not break the chain of causation. Use **Cheshire** to say Gary's act need not be the sole cause of death as long as it makes a significant contribution to it.

Gary fires a gun near Jon intending to scare him but hits him and kills him. Here there is no problem with causation so the issue is whether he intended to kill or seriously injure Jon. Apply the **Nedrick** test to decide whether the jury are likely to see death or serious injury as virtually certain and whether Gary appreciated this. You may need to refer to other facts, e.g., how close were they, was it in the open or a crowded place? Anything like this will provide evidence of how 'virtually certain' the result was and whether Gary appreciated this.

In all problem questions, you need to take a logical approach. First, read the facts carefully to ensure that you understand the points raised by the scenario. Then apply the relevant law in a logical manner, using cases in support.

Examination tip

It is **good practice** to select only the law that applies to the given facts. This shows that you understand the law well enough to know what is relevant.

It is **bad practice** to write all you know about an area just because you know it well. Even if it is right, you will gain no marks if it is not relevant to the facts given.

All exam questions can be approached in a similar way

> *identify the law*
>
> *state the law (using relevant cases)*
>
> *apply the law (using relevant cases)*
>
> *reach a conclusion (based on your application)*

Task 10 Application practice

As practice for an exam question, try this with the case of **Pagett**. Read the facts of the case and then use your knowledge of the *actus reus* and *mens rea* of murder to apply the law to these facts. Use the following as a guide.

Identify the law; a death has occurred so there is a homicide

State the law; define murder

Actus reus

> *Murder is a result crime (the result being a death), so causation is very important.*
>
> *Apply the law: Has a death been caused? Did Pagett's act cause it?*
>
> *Factual causation. State the law, using a case in support and apply this to the facts.*
>
> *Legal causation. Do the same for legal causation.*

Mens rea

> *If there is no intent it may be manslaughter but not murder, so state and apply the rules on intent.*
>
> *Identify the required intent for a murder case.*
>
> *State the test for deciding if there is intent using the appropriate case(s) in support.*
>
> *Apply it to the facts.*

Reach a conclusion based on your application.

Task 11 Application practice – from AQA examination January 2010

It is unusual for a question to be only on murder because it would be too limited. In the following scenario you are asked to discuss murder but this would then need to be developed to include the special defences to murder, i.e., voluntary manslaughter. However, as this topic is murder just answer this part of a question and ignore the defences.

Mike, Jack's father, had found it increasingly difficult to cope with the stress of modern life, including Jack's wild behaviour. Mike had developed a strong (but wholly unjustified) belief that he was being followed wherever he went, and that his life was in danger. Walking on the upper level of the shopping centre one day, he noticed Pete, who lived in the neighbourhood. Mike and Pete had recently had a number of arguments. Mike immediately assumed that Pete was "following" him, and shouted at him to go away. Pete shouted back, "If you keep on like that, someone will get you, you stupid old idiot." Pete then walked off but, a few minutes later, Mike suddenly ran at him and pushed him over the railing. Pete fell to the lower level, where he struck his head very heavily and died.

Consider the liability of Mike for the murder of Pete. (25 marks)

Task 12 Clue spotting

There is limited time in most exams and examiners rarely set a question which requires you to cover everything. To practice being selective do the following exercise.

The scenario shows that someone has died following an unlawful act by D. Look at the brief comments taken from the scenarios and add what they indicate is the focus of the question. The first one is done for you as an example.

> *Knowing the house was empty D – this suggests the focus is on mens rea; specifically whether D had intent to kill or seriously injure anyone if he believed non-one was on the premises*
>
> *V had a weak heart*
>
> *D tried to stab V in the arm but missed and hit his heart*
>
> *V was wrongly diagnosed in the hospital*
>
> *D fired at X but missed and hit Y*
>
> *V was hit by a car as she ran away*

Essay questions (evaluation)

The 'Essay pointers' and 'Key criticisms' are intended to provide you with information to use in an essay where you have to evaluate a given area of law. Look through these before doing the evaluation practice below.

This is an example of a typical exam question

'Discuss the suggestion that the current law of murder is unsatisfactory and in need of reform'
Again, a logical approach is needed. You should:

> *State what the current law is*
>
> *Identify and explain where it is unsatisfactory*
>
> *Support your comments with cases and/or examples*
>
> *Discuss where reforms are needed including any that have been proposed or implemented*

The following exercise will give you a basis for such a discussion.

Task 13 Evaluation practice

Look at the brief comments below and then:

State what the current law is, using cases where appropriate

Expand on the statement (this can be for or against it or just a brief comment of your own)

Support your comments with cases and/or examples

If reforms have been proposed or implemented, add these

There is no 'right' answer to evaluation questions, opinions vary and you can form your own – but **always** use cases and/or examples to back up what you say.

The law on intent lacks clarity

The serious harm rule should be changed

Mercy killing should be made legal

The mandatory sentence for murder should be abolished

Answers to tasks and self-test questions

Task 1

It could be argued in **Miller** that the dropping of the cigarette was a continuing act so that when he did nothing about the fire he had both *actus reus* and *mens rea*

Task 2

This task just requires you to make some notes. Keep these for revision

Task 3

The answer to this is just before the summary

Task 4

The act must be voluntary – **Leicester v Pearson**

An omission suffices if there is a duty, e.g., **Stone & Dobinson** (but there are many other cases)

The 'but for' test comes from **White**

The need for D to make a significant contribution was stated in **Cheshire**

That a foreseeable act will not break the chain of causation was stated in **Roberts**

Task 5

This task just requires you to make some notes. Keep these for revision

Self-test answers for Chapter 1

The '3 Cs' which may be included in the actus reus of a crime are

conduct

circumstances

consequences

The court found liability in **Fagan** on the basis that it was a 'continuing act'.

Two examples of when an omission can result in criminal liability are

when there is a contractual duty

when D created a dangerous situation

The thin skull rule is that D takes the victim as he or she finds them

The quote at the beginning of the Chapter came from **Pittwood**

The two types of intent are direct and indirect

The **Nedrick** test for oblique intent is

was death or serious bodily harm a virtual certainty?

did the defendant appreciate that such was the case?

The principle in **Latimer** is that malice (mens rea) can be transferred

Task 6

The answers are in the diagram following the task

Task 7

The murder charge failed in both **Nedrick and Woollin** because the jury found that D did not appreciate that death was a virtual certainty

This task just requires you to make some notes. Keep these for revision

Self-test answers for Chapter 2

The actus reus *of murder is the unlawful killing of a human being under the queen's peace. The* mens rea *has been interpreted as malice aforethought, meaning intent to kill or seriously injure.*

A result crime is one where a particular consequence is required as part of the actus reus. *Causation will therefore be important when proving* actus reus, *as D's actions must be the factual and legal cause of the result.*

*The answer depends on which cases you chose; an example would be **Nedrick**. The victim would not have died 'but for' his actions. He made a significant contribution to the death and it was foreseeable that someone could be seriously injured in an arson attack. (So he caused the death, but he was not guilty of murder because he did not have* mens rea.)

The 'virtual certainty' test for mens rea *was established in **Nedrick 1986** and confirmed by the HL in **Woollin 1998**.*

Task 9

Gibbins and Proctor –the couple intentionally withheld food from the child and this caused her death. It was murder because there was the mens rea of intent to kill or seriously injure and actus reus because their actions directly caused her death

Cheshire – by shooting him, D had significantly contributed to the man's death. Although the hospital treatment was also a contributory factor, it did not break the chain of causation because it is foreseeable that something can go wrong when treating someone who has been shot

Nedrick – D had the actus reus of murder because he caused death by setting the fire at the house. However, the evidence was that he did not appreciate that it was a virtual certainty that death or serious injury would be caused. As he did not intend to kill or seriously injure he did not have the mens rea of murder so was not guilty (he was guilty of unlawful act manslaughter)

White – D had mens rea because he intended to kill his mother with poison. However, as she died from a heart attack which was not related to the poison he had not caused her death so did not have the actus reus of murder (he was guilty of attempted murder)

Task 10 Application practice

This is a brief answer; you will need to expand a little on the cases used in support to show why they are relevant

Identify the law by reference to the fact that a death has occurred so it may be murder.

State the law. Murder is the unlawful killing of a human being under the Queen's peace with malice aforethought.

Apply the law. There is an unlawful killing but as murder is a result crime, it must be proved that **Pagett** caused the death.

Actus reus: **Factual causation.**

Factual causation is established by using the 'but for' test (**White**).

'But for' Pagett holding the girl she would not have died. He factually caused death.

Legal causation.

To prove legal causation it needs to be shown that D made a significant contribution to the death (**Cheshire**) and that nothing broke the chain of causation (**Cheshire, Roberts**).

There is a possible intervening act, that of the police. Therefore, you need apply the rules on causation to see if the chain was broken by the police firing back.

Pagett's action made a significant contribution to the girl's death by holding her in front of him. The intervening act, of the police returning fire, was foreseeable and so did not break the chain of causation (**Roberts**). He legally caused death.

Mens rea

State the law. The MR for murder is Intent to kill or seriously injure (**Smith**).

This means it was either D's aim to kill or seriously injure, (direct intent – **Mohan**), or it was a virtual certainty and D appreciated this (oblique intent – **Nedrick/Woollin**).

Apply the law. It was not Pagett's aim to kill or seriously injure the girl so there appears to be no direct intent. However if he intended to seriously injure the police when he shot at them then this intent will be enough under the doctrine of transferred malice (**Latimer**). The *mens rea* (intent to seriously injure the police) can be transferred to the *actus reus* (the death of the girl).

If direct intent cannot be proved then apply the rules on oblique intent. The jury will need to decide if death or serious injury was a 'virtual certainty'. This is debateable. The jury will also have to decide whether they believe Pagett himself (a subjective test) appreciated it to be a virtual certainty – again debateable.

In conclusion, Pagett could be found guilty of murder but this charge may not succeed due to the difficulty of proving *mens rea* (but he will be guilty of manslaughter, as was the case).

Exam pointer

It is acceptable to say 'could be' or 'probably' in your conclusions to exam questions on a problem scenario (although if studying with OCR the short statements will require a more definite answer as to whether they are accurate). There is rarely a definite answer, especially if it is a decision for a jury. You can see this is true by the conflicting decisions you come across. However, you should always attempt a conclusion and if there is doubt move on to an alternative offence. In a scenario like this, you would need to go on to explain and apply the law on unlawful act manslaughter. You would also need to discuss any possible and relevant defences as appropriate.

From AQA examination January 2010

Murder is the unlawful killing of a human being. Mike pushed Pete over the railing which is unlawful and caused Pete's death, so this appears to fulfil the *actus reus*. On the given facts, causation is not an issue. The main issue is *mens rea*. The *mens rea* of murder is intent to kill or seriously injure (**Smith**). As death or serious injury is probably not Mike's aim or purpose, as described in **Mohan**, it may be hard to prove direct intent, but indirect intent is possible. The law on indirect intent comes from **Nedrick** and was confirmed by the House of Lords in **Woollin**. Death or serious injury as a result of D's actions must be a virtual certainty, and D must appreciate this. It is a virtual certainty that if a person is pushed and falls from the upper level of a shopping centre, they will be at least be seriously injured if not die. If the jury 'find' that Mike appreciated this then he has the necessary *mens rea* for murder, as in **Matthews & Alleyne** where the D's pushed someone in a river knowing he could not swim. It is arguable either way because Mike was delusional so even though the first part of the test is satisfied the second part is more doubtful. The jury may well believe that Mike did not appreciate that death or serious injury was a virtual certainty. However, if *mens rea* is established he may be able to use a partial defence to the murder charge.

Task 12 Clue spotting

Knowing the house was empty – this suggests the focus is on *mens rea*; specifically indirect intent and that D must appreciate that death or serious injury was a virtual certainty which may not be the case if he believed no one was on the premises (**Nedrick**)

V had a weak heart – this suggests the focus is on the thin skull rule; specifically that D is liable for the full consequences if V dies even if a normal healthy person would not have done (**Blaue**)

D tried to stab V in the arm but missed and hit his heart – this suggests the focus is on *mens rea*; specifically that intent to seriously is sufficient and it is not necessary to prove intent to kill (**DPP v Smith**)

V was wrongly diagnosed in the hospital – this suggests the focus is on causation; specifically that hospital treatment rarely breaks the chain of causation as long as D made a significant contribution to the death (**Cheshire**)

D fired at X but missed and hit Y – this suggests the focus is on transferred malice; specifically that the *mens rea* of intending to kill or seriously injure X can be transferred to the *actus reus* of killing Y (**Latimer**)

V was hit by a car as she ran away from D's attack – this suggests the focus is on causation; specifically that a foreseeable act by the victim will not break the chain of causation (**Roberts**)

Task 13 Evaluation practice

The following are just a few ideas; you may have other equally valid criticisms. Build up a few ideas like this and you will soon have a sound base which you can develop for an essay/evaluation question

The law on intent lacks clarity

The current law is that intent can be found if D appreciated that death or serious injury was a virtually certain result (**Nedrick/Woollin**). Use the cases on the development of the law on intent to show the different definitions used by judges over the years. These can support a discussion of whether there is/has been a lack of clarity. Is the law more satisfactory since **Nedrick/Woollin**? Use the quote from Lord Hope in **Woollin** to support any comment saying that it is clearer now (examiners like to see examples and quotes in support as well as cases, and a criticism of the law should always recognise any positive changes). However, **Walker & Hayles** can be used to suggest it is still not sufficiently clear.

The serious harm rule should be changed

Discuss whether it is right that someone can be convicted of murder where the intent is to cause serious harm rather than death, which is the current law – **DPP v Smith**. The rule was confirmed in **Cunningham 1981** and although the Law Lords criticised it, they refused to overrule it, preferring to leave that to Parliament. The Law Commission has also criticised it and in their report, *Murder, Manslaughter and Infanticide* suggest splitting murder into first and second degree, as in the United States. If there were only intent to cause serious harm, it would be second-degree murder with a discretionary sentence.

The Law Commission gives an example of D punching someone who falls and hits their head and dies of a brain haemorrhage. The act is wrong, but it is debateable whether it should be murder. This is particularly controversial in light of the thin skull rule. Splitting murder into first and second degree would seem fairer.

However, the rule is that D must intend *serious* harm, so perhaps it should be murder in such a case, at least until the Commission's proposals are accepted (of which there is no sign).

Mercy killing should be made legal

Euthanasia or 'mercy killing' is controversial. Under the current law, killing someone who is suffering and begs for relief from the pain will be murder, as the aim or purpose is to kill, so there will be direct intent. This intentional act has caused death, so it is murder. The same would apply to a doctor who took positive action to end someone's life. Although an omission to act has been held by the courts not to be murder – **Airedale NHS Trust v Bland**, this seems to be a decision based on morality rather than law as many people would see turning off life-support as an act so strictly (and legally) speaking it should be murder. The huge contrast in sentencing in the cases of **Inglis** and **Gilderdale** highlight the problems; one was given life and the other a suspended sentence but they had both killed their child. It is arguable that it should be up to Parliament, as elected by the people, to clarify the law and not leave it to the courts where judicial decisions may be inconsistent and where juries may well convict or acquit for ethical rather than legal reasons.

(*Many of the cases seen with diminished responsibility involve mercy killing, so you can add voluntary manslaughter cases to this argument.*)

The mandatory sentence for murder should be abolished

There are valid arguments for and against the current law that all murder convictions result in a life sentence. Murder is very serious so a life sentence can be said to be appropriate. However, there are different degrees of violence involved in murder cases and it seems wrong that all intentional killings attract the same sentence. The DPP and the Law Commission have both recommended that there should not be a mandatory life sentence and that it should be discretionary. This would allow judges to consider the particular circumstances when sentencing. Currently they can only make a recommendation of what 'life' should mean as a minimum or maximum. The LC recommended a three-tier structure for homicide, which would cover 1st-degree murder, 2nd-degree murder and manslaughter. Only the first of these would have a mandatory life sentence. You could also point out that the reforms suggested by the Law Commission on murder have not been accepted so the law of murder is still based on decisions by judges rather than Parliament. This in itself can be said to be unsatisfactory for such a serious offence.

Examination tip

As voluntary manslaughter only applies to a murder charge, any question about the law on murder could include discussions of the problems and reforms of this area too.

Appendix: Abbreviations

The following abbreviations are commonly used. You may use them in an examination answer, but write them in full the first time, e.g., write 'actual bodily harm (ABH)' and then after that you can just write 'ABH'.

General

Draft Code – A Criminal Code for England and Wales (Law Commission No. 177), 1989

CCRC Criminal Cases Review Commission

ABH actual bodily harm

GBH grievous bodily harm

D defendant

C claimant

V Victim

CA Court of Appeal

HL House of Lords

SC Supreme Court

Acts

S – section (thus **s 1** Theft Act 1968 refers to section 1 of that Act)

s 1(2) means section 1 subsection 2 of an Act

OAPA – Offences against the Person Act 1861

In cases – these don't need to be written in full

CC (at beginning) chief constable

CC (at end) county council

BC borough council

DC district council

LBC London borough council

AHA Area Health Authority

J Justice

LJ Lord Justice

LCJ Lord Chief Justice

LC Lord Chancellor

AG Attorney General

CPS Crown Prosecution Service

DPP Director of Public Prosecutions

AG Attorney General